13
ALT

D1151269

VICTORIA & ALBERT MUSEUM

Ham House

LONDON 1976

CONTENTS

© Crown copyright 1968

Fourth edition 1976

ISBN 0 901486 95 7

Printed in England for Her Majesty's Stationery Office
by W & J Mackay Ltd Dd 326772 K480 1/77

INTRODUCTION

Ham House is remarkable because it presents us with more aspects of 17th century life than any other house in the country.

Apart from the fact that its architectural fabric has been preserved virtually unchanged since the 1670s (when the building was enlarged and re-organized by the Duke and Duchess of Lauderdale), it still contains almost all its furnishings from that period—and that is a most exceptional phenomenon. Moreover, the gardens have been so little altered since then that it is currently proving possible to restore them to their original guise.

As a result, we can still obtain a clear impression of this house as a complete entity, the grounds constituting an ordered extension of the house and its carefully planned interior.

Ancient houses reveal themselves only gradually. As we study them more and our fund of information is built up, so our understanding of their significance and complexity deepens and changes. There is no finality in these matters; thus the arrangements of the rooms at Ham House are continually being adjusted, always, we hope, the better to convey the intentions and aspirations of the Lauderdales and Dysarts, their architects and decorators. For we believe it is into such matters that many of those who visit our 'stately homes' seek an insight, and there is nowhere that they can do so better than at Ham House.

We hope, therefore, that the public will not feel aggrieved if they find objects have been moved from time to time; this is a direct reflection of our developing understanding of the principles of room arrangement and its nuances. We try to bring out new editions of the guide to cover these alterations but it has never proved possible to gear publication to such developments precisely. Each successive edition summarizes the current state of our knowledge as it pertains to this particular house—indeed, a reading of the various editions will one day reveal much about changing attitudes to the presentation of country houses, which springs from the rapidly growing interest that has become increasingly apparent since the War.

This edition, like the former two, has been compiled by Mr Maurice Tomlin under my general supervision and in collaboration with our colleagues.

The house and its gardens were generously given to the National Trust in 1948 by the late Sir Lyonel Tollemache, Bt, and his son, Mr Cecil Tollemache, whose ancestors had inhabited the house for three centuries. To ensure proper maintenance of the property, the National Trust made it over on a long lease to the Ministry of Works, while the contents were purchased by the Government and entrusted to the care of the Victoria and Albert Museum, which is responsible for the administration of the house. We are much indebted to Major-General Sir Humphry Tollemache, C.B.E., D.L., for allowing us to quote from the building accounts of the 1670s, which are among his family papers.

PETER THORNTON
Keeper, Department of Furniture and Woodwork
1976

OUTLINE HISTORY

Ham House was built in 1610 by Sir Thomas Vavasour, Knight Marshal to James I. Certain alterations, notably the building of the new Great Staircase, were made by William Murray, 1st Earl of Dysart, between 1637 and 1639. But the house as it appears today is largely the creation of his daughter, Elizabeth, and her second husband, the Duke of Lauderdale. During the 1670s, having employed the architect William Samwell to enlarge the house by adding a new suite of rooms along the South Front on each floor (see plans on pp. 8–9), they furnished the interior with a luxuriousness that was remarkable even in that lavish age. Most of the furniture at Ham today dates from that period.

The only other significant alterations since the time of the Lauderdales were made by the 4th Earl of Dysart, who acquired some fine new furniture shortly after inheriting the title in 1727 and was also responsible for certain architectural alterations, which included the installation of the existing sash windows.

It seems that much of the original furniture was stored away for long periods. Consequently, although Time has had its inevitable effect, so that the original window-curtains and many of the wall-hangings no longer exist, the interior of the house still presents much of its sumptuous 17th century appearance and still vividly recalls the 'politer way of living' introduced after the Restoration, which 'soon passed to luxury and intolerable expense'.

(For a more detailed history of the house, see p. 48.)

Several inventories of the contents of the house survive. In most cases the old names for the rooms have been retained and the furniture and pictures have been replaced as far as possible in their original positions. The arrangements revealed by the inventory of 1679 have been adopted in most cases but it has occasionally been necessary to seek guidance from the later ones.

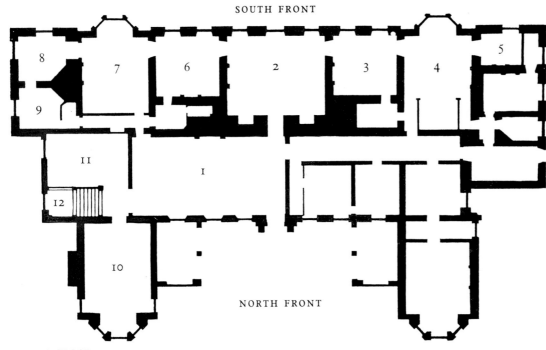

SOUTH FRONT

NORTH FRONT

GROUND FLOOR

1 Great Hall
2 Marble Dining Room
3 Duke's Dressing Room
4 Duchess's Bedchamber
5 Duke's Closet
6 Withdrawing Room

7 Yellow Bedchamber or Volury Room
8 White Closet
9 Duchess's Private Closet
10 Chapel
11 Inner Hall
12 Great Staircase

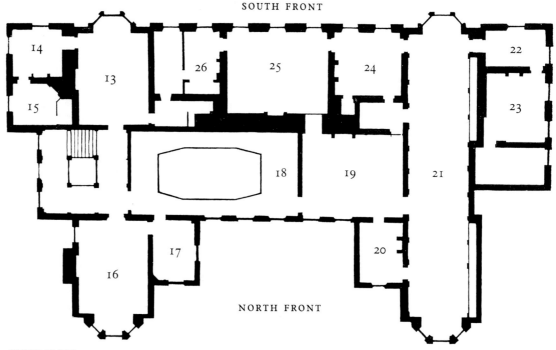

SOUTH FRONT

NORTH FRONT

FIRST FLOOR

13 Lady Maynard's Chamber
14 Lady Maynard's Dressing Room
15 Bedchamber Within
16 Room over the Chapel (Museum Room)
17 Cabinet of Miniatures
18 Round Gallery
19 North Drawing Room

20 Green Closet
21 Long Gallery
22 Library Closet
23 Library
24 Antechamber to the Queen's Bedchamber
25 Queen's Bedchamber
26 Queen's Closet

TOUR OF THE HOUSE

Denotes items lent by the Victoria and Albert Museum. Although the policy is to exhibit only furniture that is original to the house, a few exceptions have been made in order to complete the furnishing of certain rooms.

THE GREAT HALL

In the original H-shaped house of 1610 this room (corresponding with the horizontal bar in the letter 'H') had a window on the right of the fireplace. The opening of the front door into one end of the Hall and the disposing of the service rooms at the other side show the surviving influence of the traditional medieval house-plan, where the entrance would have led into a screens passage at one end of the hall. The raised section of floor at the far end of the Hall, however, is not a dais, as was formerly supposed, but merely marks the original position of the wall at that end before the room was enlarged in the 1630s. The ceiling originally continued right across, the octagonal opening having been made early in the 18th century.

In 1679 the Hall contained little more than a billiard table and two benches and, on the walls, a collection of firearms and other weapons together with a large map of England, two drums and 24 leather firebuckets (now in the West Passage). The Hall is now furnished with the mahogany side-tables and oak hall-chairs bearing the arms of the Tollemache family that were installed by the 4th Earl of Dysart in about 1730. The two figures over the fireplace are believed to represent William Murray, 1st Earl of Dysart, and his wife, dressed as Mars and Minerva. They were possibly modelled by Francesco Fanelli, a sculptor from the court circle of Charles I (active c. 1609–c. 1665), who may also have executed the bronze fitments on the chimney-piece below.

The paintings (clockwise from the left of the fireplace):

Lyonel Tollemache, 4th Earl of Dysart (1708–70) by John Vanderbank (1694–1739).

Grace Carteret, Countess of Dysart (1713–55) by John Vanderbank.

Charlotte Walpole, Countess of Dysart (1738–89) by Sir Joshua Reynolds (1723–92). Exhibited at the Royal Academy in 1775.

Louisa Manners, Countess of Dysart (1745–1840) by John Hoppner (1758–1810), after Reynolds. The original (exhibited at the Royal Academy in 1779) is now in the Iveagh Bequest at Kenwood.

Sir Lionel Tollemache, 1st Bart. (1562?–1621). Artist unknown.

Henrietta Cavendish (d. 1717. Wife of Lyonel, Lord Huntingtower, grandson of the Duchess of Lauderdale) by Sir Godfrey Kneller (1646–1723).

1. (*right*)
Great Hall (*National Trust*)

James Stuart, Duke of Lennox and Richmond (1612–55) after Sir Anthony Van Dyck (1599–1641). The original is in the Metropolitan Museum, New York.

Called *The Marchioness of Winchester* (2nd wife of the 5th Marquess) after Van Dyck. The original has not been traced.

Visitors who wish to see a short introductory slide show before continuing the tour of the house should go through the doorway to the left of the Front Door, continuing along the West Passage to the Demonstration Room.

THE MARBLE DINING ROOM

This is the central room, on either side of which are disposed symmetrically the apartments of the Duke and Duchess of Lauderdale—the whole constituting the Domestic Floor, where the family lived, whereas the principal rooms on the first floor were State Rooms intended for grand occasions and for show. The grounds are laid out on an axis which passes through the centre of this room, extending across the grass parterres, leading through the middle of the Wilderness to the South Gate and continuing by the South Avenue to Ham Common.

The room originally had a floor of black and white marble; the present very fine parquetry floor probably dates from the second quarter of the 18th

2. Marble
Dining Room
(*National Trust*)

century. The gilt-leather wall-hangings are mentioned in the inventories of the Lauderdale period; it is most unusual to find panels of this once-popular form of wall-covering in their original position. The carved details were carried out by John Bullimore in 1672/73; for the 'bunches of leaves about ye dores' he charged 2s per foot.

The furniture in 1679 consisted of two cedar side-tables, three oval tables, also of cedar, a marble cistern, a clock in a walnut case and 18 carved walnut chairs with cane seats. By 1683 two 'chayres for children, the one black and the other japanned' had been added.

The cedar side-tables still stand in the recesses and one of the chairs has survived (on the fireplace side of the entrance doorway); the oval folding table is also an original Ham piece. The rest of the chairs★ and the clock★, signed *Joseph Knibb London*, help to complete the furnishing of the room as it was in 1679. The chairs have been arranged around the walls in a formal manner, as was the custom when they were not in use. (Two of the folding tables would have stood in the window recesses, where the radiators are now.) The cistern, or wine-cooler, stands under one of the side-tables at which the diners' glasses would have been filled. The very fine gilded pier-glasses date from about 1730.

Inset paintings:

Four of the overdoor paintings are 17th century copies of a series of playing boys by Polidoro Caldara (Roman School, d. 1543), acquired by Charles I in 1637 and now at Hampton Court Palace. The same boys, satyrs and goats served as models for those in the paintings with which Francis Cleyn (1582–1658) decorated the cove and ceiling of the Green Closet upstairs (see p. 35).

Over the middle door: *A Fantastic Landscape* by a follower of Hieronymus Bosch.

Over the fireplace: *Rose, the Royal Gardener, presenting Charles II with the first Pineapple grown in England*. After the well-known painting attributed to Henry Danckerts (c. 1625–c. 1679) in the collection of the Marchioness of Cholmondeley at Houghton Hall. An inscription on the back states that it was copied by Thomas Hewart, aged twenty, in October 1787.

Turning to the right, the visitor enters:

THE DUKE'S DRESSING ROOM

The modern damask wall-hangings are copied from a material at Hampton Court woven for William III. The ebonized table and candlestands, carved in the so-called Auricular style, are believed to have been made in Holland in about 1670. The other table, which is probably also Dutch, is decorated with an imitation of Chinese incised lacquer. The chairs that stood in this room have not survived and those seen here now are part of a large set made about 1730. Their modern protective covers are of the type that would have been used at that time.

Inset paintings:

Over the fireplace: *A Battle-Piece* by Jan Wyck (1640–1702).

Over the doors: *Two Landscapes with Classical Ruins* by Henry Danckerts; one signed 'H.D. 1673.'

Hanging paintings:

Charles Maitland, 3rd Earl of Lauderdale (c. 1620–91); brother of the Duke of Lauderdale. Artist unknown.

Danae and the Shower of Gold after Hans Rottenhammer (1564–1625).

Classical Ruins with the Figures of Christ and the Woman of Canaan by Bartholomeus Breenbergh (1599/1600–?1656). Signed and dated 1635. Dutch School.

St Sebastian. Italian School.

Orpheus charming the Animals after Jacopo Bassano (1510–92).

Bacchanalian Scene attributed to H. van Balen (1575–1632).

THE DUCHESS'S BEDCHAMBER

This was the Duke's Bedchamber when the first alterations were made to the house in the 1670s and his Dressing Room and Closet are next door but it was clearly the Duchess's room by 1675, while he had moved into *her* old bedchamber (see p. 18), which is next to her two closets. The move may have been occasioned by her need for more extensive accommodation for her lady-in-waiting (in rooms behind the scenes, not open to the public) and by the provision of a bathroom in the basement below.

The room was originally hung with crimson and gold damask. The artificial graining and partial gilding of the wooden panelling which is seen here and in several other rooms at Ham House is an interesting feature, dating from the 1670s. The bill from the carver, John Bullimore, dated April 1673, includes an item for '33 ft of great rafle leaves at 1s. 8d.' This was for the moulding framing the alcove. The curtains are modern reproductions, based on descriptions of the originals.

As far as possible the room has been furnished as it was when the 1679 inventory was drawn up. However, the original bed, which had a 'Counterpane of Crimson and gold colour damusk' and 'foure cups and spriggs (urn-like finials with plumes) for ye top of ye bed' has not survived. The present bed* dates from about 1730 and is probably rather taller than the original. The curtains and coverlet are modern reproductions, based on the surviving material, which can still be seen at the bed head and on the tester.

3. *Sea-piece* by Willem van de Velde the Younger

The cabinet is veneered with kingwood and there is a similarly decorated strong box, which was described in the 17th century as a 'box with an extraordinary lock' (which indeed it has). The brass-bound jewel-case also belonged to the Duchess but was supplied with a new stand in the 18th century. The clock*, signed *John Knibb, Oxon*, dates from about 1700.

The pole-screen with silver mounts is an early example of its type, though the tapestry panel is a later replacement. The tongs and shovel are similarly mounted with silver; this silver chimney-furniture, which is a feature of several of the rooms, has long been a celebrated curiosity and strikingly testifies to the Lauderdales' luxurious taste. It was in allusion to such ostentation that John Evelyn (or his daughter, Mary), in a satire on the follies of the time wrote,

The chimney furniture of plate
For irons now quite out of date[1]

Most of the fireplaces have their original iron firebacks; the plain delftware tiles are also original.

Inset paintings:

Over the bed: The ceiling, painted in oil on plaster, is in the style of Antonio Verrio (1639?–1707).

Over the doors: Four *Sea-Pieces* by Willem van

[1] *Mundus Muliebris, or The Ladies' Dressing Room Unlock'd & her Toilet Spread*, 1690.

15

de Velde the Younger (1633–1707). All are signed; the smaller ones are dated *London 1673*. These pictures must have been specially commissioned from the artist, who had just arrived in England from Holland. The places assigned to them above the doors are unfavourable to paintings of this quality, which may explain why they have only in recent years been recognized as authentic and admirable works of one of the greatest marine painters.[1] The art in which Van de Velde excelled was that of painting ships rather than the sea itself; for this reason his 'calms' show him to greater advantage than his 'storms', since a smooth sea offers greater scope for this kind of marine portraiture. In this room are two examples of each (pl. 3).

These pictures, which have distinctly masculine connotations, were painted before the Duke relinquished this room as his bedchamber.

Hanging paintings:

Over the fireplace: *The Duke of Lauderdale*, in crayons, by Edmund Ashfield (active c. 1670–1700). Signed and dated 1674–75 (pl. 27).

Opposite the fireplace: *Elizabeth Dysart* (later Duchess of Lauderdale) *with her first Husband,*

[1] They are not included in the comprehensive list of the artist's works by Hofsteede de Groote in his *Catalogue of Dutch painters.*

4. *Elizabeth Dysart with her first husband, Sir Lyonel Tollemache, and her sister, Lady Maynard.* Attributed to Joan Carlile

Sir Lyonel Tollemache, and her Sister, Lady Maynard, attributed to Joan Carlile (1606?–79) (pl. 4). This is a 'conversation piece'; examples of so early a date (c. 1648) painted in England are very rare. The frame is of later date.

THE DUKE'S CLOSET

Hung in the 17th century with black and gold damask, the walls of this little room have recently been covered with a modern damask and trimmings in the same colour scheme.

The remarkable writing-cabinet, veneered with burr elm and ebony and embellished with silver mounts, was described in the 1679 inventory as a 'scriptor garnished with silver'; traces of silvering can be seen on the legs of the stand. In the 17th century the room also contained two side chairs and 'one Sleeping Chayre of Crimson velvet with crimson & gold fring'. (The pair of 'Sleeping chayres' that was in the Queen's Closet still survives—see p. 47.)
Inset paintings:

Over the fireplace: *An Alchemist* signed Thomas Wyck (1616–77).

Below this: *A Sea-Piece* assigned to Van de Velde in the 1683 inventory.

The ceiling, painted in oil on plaster: *Two Female Figures representing Music* in the style of Antonio Verrio.

5. Chair covered with figured velvet; about 1730

Hanging paintings:

Charles Maitland, 3rd Earl of Lauderdale by David Paton (worked c. 1660–1695. Indian ink).

An Alchemist by Thomas Wyck (1616–77).

Sir Thomas Delves, Bart. (1630–1713) attributed to Mary Beale (1632–97).

St Anthony. Italian School.

Hagar and Ishmael after P. F. Mola (1612–66).

Returning through the Marble Dining Room, the visitor reaches:

THE WITHDRAWING ROOM

This room now contains furniture dating from the 1730s, the period when the 4th Earl of Dysart carried out a considerable amount of refurnishing at Ham. The seat furniture (pl. 5), made of fruitwood, forms part of a large suite covered in red and green figured velvet which was probably made at Spitalfields. The pier-glass between the windows, dating from nearer the middle of the century, is surmounted by a winged horse, the crest of the Tollemache family.
Inset paintings:

Over the doors: Two more copies of the Polidoros at Hampton Court.

Over the fireplace: *Plants, Insects and a Squirrel* by A. C. Bega (1637–97).

Hanging paintings:

Frances, Lady Worsley (1673–1750). Grandmother

of Grace Carteret, Countess of Dysart. Attributed to Charles d'Agar (1669–1723).

Sir Robert Worsley (1669–1747). Artist unknown. Dated 1693.

Wilbraham, 6th Earl of Dysart (?) (1739–1821). Possibly by Philip Mercier (1689–1760).

Wilbraham, 6th Earl of Dysart as a Child. Artist unknown.

THE YELLOW BEDCHAMBER OR VOLURY ROOM

In an inventory drawn up about 1651 this was referred to as being the Bedchamber of Elizabeth Dysart (later Duchess of Lauderdale) By 1677 it had come to be called the Yellow Bedchamber on account of its yellow damask wall-hangings; at about this time the Duchess moved to the bedroom at the other end of the South Front and the Duke apparently took over this room until his death in 1682. According to an inventory drawn up in the following year, the bed and certain other items of furniture had been removed and the room had acquired the name of 'Volury Roome' (the word is apparently derived from the French *volière* or *volerie*; bird-cages are known to have been erected outside the bay-windows but it is also possible that birds were actually housed in the room during the winter).

In spite of her change-over to the bedroom at the other end of the house, the Duchess still retained her two Closets adjacent to her former bedchamber, in the same way as the Duke kept his ancillary rooms—seemingly a somewhat awkward arrangement.

The 'black & yellow vain'd chimney in my Lady's Chamber' was installed by the mason, John Lampen, in 1672 at a cost of £15.

The bed, which comes from another room, has modern hangings, although some of the original materials may still be seen on the dome. The purple-and-yellow colour scheme of the bed has governed our restoration of the whole room, which now has hangings and chair-covers *en suite*—as they would have been in the 17th century. The original colours in this room were in fact yellow and blue. The chairs are part of a set of ten which belong here. (A pair must have stood flanking the windows, where the 18th century tables and pier-glasses are now.) Also here was the cabinet decorated with panels of red tortoiseshell, which has an elaborate architectural interior; it was probably made in Antwerp in the 1630s. The porcelain* here, as in most of the rooms, is Chinese, of the K'ang Hsi period (1662–1722).

On the left of the bed is a concealed door for servants.

Inset paintings:

Two paintings of birds by the English artist Francis Barlow (1626 ?–1702), well-known for his drawings and paintings of wild life and field sports;

one is signed and dated 1673. These paintings of birds, which are more appropriate for a lady's bedchamber, were installed when the room was still occupied by the Duchess.

Hanging paintings:

Faun and Bacchante after Rubens.

The Israelites gathering Manna. School of Bassano.

John Maitland, 1st Earl of Lauderdale (d. 1645); father of the Duke of Lauderdale. Artist unknown.

Boors Smoking and Drinking after Adriaen Brouwer (1606–38).

Boors Playing at Cards. Artist unknown.

A Mediterranean Seaport by Thomas Wyck.

THE WHITE CLOSET

This richly decorated little room and the Private Closet beyond formed part of the Duchess's original apartment before she moved to the bedchamber at the other end of the house and she retained these two rooms for her personal use. This closet was decorated in the most advanced taste of the day and was largely for show. The wall-hangings and portières are modern reconstructions, based on careful interpretations of the original inventory descriptions.

In 1679 the room contained:

One Scriptore of princewood garnished with silver. This is the little writing cabinet veneered with oysterwork, made of what today is known as 'kingwood' (pl. 7).

One little cedar table. This has not survived.

Six arme chayres Japand, with black cane bottomes. These have not survived. The 'japanned backstool' seen here now, some of which were in her Private Closet, next door, in the 17th century, is designed in a naïve attempt to reproduce an Oriental form. These bear on their cresting a coronet and the Duchess's cypher E.D. (for Elizabeth Dysart). Unlike most late 17th century chairs, they are decorated behind, suggesting that they were probably grouped informally, rather than placed around the walls of the room as was the normal custom. No doubt they were often used for the fashionable pastime of tea-drinking, for which their Oriental appearance would have made them particularly appropriate.

One brasse head over the Chimney. This refers to the bust of the Duchess's mother, Catherine Bruce, Countess of Dysart, which has recently been cleaned to reveal the original gilding underneath. It has been ascribed to Hubert le Seuer but is more likely to be by the Italian, Francesco Fanelli, like the figures in the Hall.

One Indian furnace for tee garnished with Silver. This has not survived.

Inset paintings:

Over the fireplace: *Ham House from the South* attributed to Henry Danckerts. This shows the

6. Ceiling of the White Closet.
By Antonio Verrio

7. 'Scriptor'
with kingwood
oysterwork and
silver mounts

formal garden lay-out very clearly. (Front cover.)
Over the doors: two *Landscapes with Figures and Cattle* by Dirck van den Bergen.
The ceiling painting by Verrio.
Hanging paintings:
A West Indian Plantation by Franz Post (c. 1612–80).
A Landscape signed B. Breenbergh (1599/1600–1656?).
Peasant with a Jug. School of Teniers.
Wooded Landscape possibly by Jan Wynants (c. 1625–84).
Head of St Paul by Benedetto Gennari (1633–1715).
The Holy Family by David Paton, after Andrea del Sarto.
Portrait of a Youth aged 18 in 1546. Italian School.

THE DUCHESS'S PRIVATE CLOSET

The furniture in the Duchess's time consisted of a scriptor, a 'Japan box for Sweetmeats and tea', 'Six Japan'd backstooles with Cane bottomes', two sets of japanned bookshelves, a carved and gilded tea-table and two other small tables. Some of the japanned chairs with cane seats can still be seen here and the scriptor, tea-table and incised lacquer box may well be the ones referred to in the 17th century inventories. The table, which comes from Java, has had a lower stage added after its arrival in this country, in order to bring it to a more convenient height.

Inset paintings:

Over the door: *Classical Ruins* by William Gowe Ferguson (1632/3– after 1695; see p. 65).

Over the fireplace: *A Sorceress among Classical Ruins* by the same artist.

The allegorical ceiling painting depicting Fortitude surrounded by figures symbolizing Time, Death and Eternity is attributed to Verrio.

Hanging paintings:

The Baptism of Christ by Abraham Bloemart (1564–c. 1651). Dutch School. This was here in the Duchess's time.

Salome with the Head of St John the Baptist by Jacques Stellaert, also known as Stella (1596–1657). Signed and dated 1637. French School.

The Virgin and Child with St John the Baptist by the same artist.

On the scriptor: *Catherine Bruce, Countess of Dysart* by John Hoskins (d. 1664). Signed and dated 1638. This was here in the Duchess's time.

According to the 1679 inventory this room contained 23 pictures (other than insets), most of them being miniatures or very small paintings.

THE CHAPEL

This was created by the Lauderdales. The furniture and carved details were supplied by the joiner, Henry Harlow, in 1673 and 1674. The altar cloth of 'crimson velvet & gould & silver stuff with gould & silver fringe' still drapes the original table; such coverings are now of the utmost rarity. The alms dish and candlesticks,* of Flemish origin, are of a form commonly used on the altar in Anglican churches at that period.

THE INNER HALL

The furniture shown here all dates from about the middle of the 18th century. The armchairs (pl. 8) are remarkable in that they are still upholstered in the original woollen cut velvet—a material particularly susceptible to attack by moths. The harpsichord is dated 1634 and bears the name of the celebrated maker Johannes Ruckers of Antwerp but it is now believed to have been made in London around 1730. 17th century Flemish harpsichords, particularly those of the Ruckers establishment, were in great demand on account of their excellent musical qualities, right through the 18th century. Makers in London and Paris commonly adapted these ancient instruments to the extended musical requirements of their day and this harpsichord, with its spurious inscription, appears to be masquerading as a stretched instrument of this kind, although it was presumably entirely new when acquired.

8. (*right*)
Armchair covered with woollen velvet; mid-18th century

The paintings:

William, 2nd Duke of Hamilton, with the Earl (later Duke) of Lauderdale by Cornelius Johnson (1593–1664?). Signed and dated 1649. A replica is at Lennoxlove in the collection of the Duke of Hamilton. Johnson was an artist of Flemish origin, born in London, who between 1620 and 1643 painted a series of English portraits, many of them remarkable for delicacy of perception, and then withdrew to Holland to avoid the Civil War. In 1649 Lauderdale and Hamilton were both in Holland with Charles II. This painting, like all the others here and on the Staircase, has a fine carved frame but it is the only one to have been gilded.

The Angel appearing to the Shepherds after Abraham Bloemart (1564–c. 1651).

The Battle of Lepanto attributed to Cornelius Vroom (1590/1–1661). Dutch School.

A Starling with Cherries. Artist unknown.

THE GREAT STAIRCASE

Constructed in 1637 or 1638, this handsome staircase is an early example of a type which reached its fullest development after the Restoration—a staircase in which the balustrade is composed of carved and pierced panels instead of balusters. In the earliest of such staircases, dating from towards the

23

9. Detail of the
Great Staircase

end of James I's reign, the panels are pierced with strap-work designs, while those constructed after the middle of the century are mostly ornamented with continuous scroll-work. The boldly carved trophies of arms at Ham are very unusual.

A plasterer named Joseph Kinsman decorated the ceiling between 1637 and 1638 for William Murray, the Duchess's father. His bill describes the work done as follows:

Imprimis the frete[1] Sealing on the head of the new great staires containing 68 yards at 7s a yard

£23. 16. 0.

For the frete under the said staires containing 86 yards at 3s 6d a yard £15. 1. 0.

Thomas Carter, the joiner, charged £6 for making 'the great arch' between the hall and the staircase, £7 for 24 yards of wainscot on the stairs, £4 16s for six windows with their mouldings, and £45 in all for five pairs of doors with their cases and 'frontispieces'. There is no mention of the stairs themselves, but it is clear from the reference, quoted above, to the 'new great stairs' that they were constructed at the same date. Mathew Goodriche's account shows that he charged £64 in all for painting and partly gilding the woodwork.[2]

[1]Fret (also frette, frete), noun = (in architectural sense), ornamental work in relief, especially on ceilings. Obsolete.

Most of the wood was painted and 'veined' to imitate walnut, but some of the carved ornament was originally gilded. The staircase was restored in 1960. It is hoped shortly to repaint the walls in their original red colour.

The paintings:

Landscape with Cattle by Dirck van den Bergen (1640–95). Signed *D.V.B.* Dutch School.

Diana with Nymphs by Adrian van Nieulandt (1587–1658). Signed and dated 1615. Dutch School.

Diana and Actaeon after an original by Titian in the Earl of Ellesmere's collection.

Cupid, Mercury and Psyche after Corregio.

Venus and Adonis after the original by Titian in the National Gallery.

Julius Caesar sending his Despatches to Rome by Jacob de Gheyn II (1565–1629).

Venus and the Organ Player after an original by Titian in the Prado, Madrid.

LADY MAYNARD'S CHAMBER

Lady Maynard, the Duchess's sister, occupied this room in 1679 but after her death in 1682 Lord Huntingtower, the Duchess's son, moved in. The

[2]Goodriche was assistant to John De Critz the Elder, Serjeant Painter to Charles I.

Jacobean-style oak frieze is not original to the room and probably dates from the first half of the 19th century. The tapestries are late 17th century Flemish work after paintings by Nicholas Poussin in the Louvre depicting incidents in the life of Pyrrhus, King of Epirus, during the 3rd century B.C.

The room is now furnished approximately as it was in the early 19th century, when the chairs and stools and a bed were installed, all fitted with the yellow satin decorated with couched red cord to be seen here now (the bedstead itself is modern). The chairs are believed to have been made in 1813, reproducing the design of a set of 17th century chairs that may be seen elsewhere in the house, but with their proportions slightly altered so that the early 18th century yellow and red covers could be used on them. (One of these covers—still unused—can be seen in the Museum Room.) The stools and firescreen were made at the same time as the chairs.

The very fine marquetry looking-glass (pl. 10), which closely resembles one at Windsor Castle, dates from the time of the Lauderdales and was here in the early 19th century, as was the table *en suite*; the original pair of candlestands belonging to the set has long since disappeared. The 18th century lacquer chest was also in this room at the time.

Inset paintings:

Two *Landscapes with Cattle* by Dirck van den Bergen.

10. Looking-glass with marquetry frame

LADY MAYNARD'S DRESSING ROOM

Inset paintings:
  Two *Landscapes* by Dirck van den Bergen.
Hanging paintings:
  Two early commissions by John Constable:
  Maria Lewis, Countess of Dysart (d. 1804) after Sir Joshua Reynolds and *Louisa Manners, Countess of Dysart* (1745–1840) after John Hoppner. Constable stayed several times at Ham and became intimate with the family. He copied other portraits for them and in allusion to such tasks wrote in 1812: 'I am making sad ravages of my time with the wretched portraits I mentioned to you. I am ungallant enough to be alluding to the Ladies' portraits.'[1]
  Capt. the Hon. John Tollemache, R.N. (d. 1779). Artist unknown.

THE BEDCHAMBER WITHIN

This was presumably used by Lady Maynard's companion or personal maidservant. The furniture shown here now includes an English commode of about 1785, made in the French Transitional style. It still has its original leather cover; such covers were frequently provided for the protection of furniture

[1] C. R. Leslie, *Memoirs of the Life of John Constable*, ed. Hon. A. Shirley, 1937, p. 54.

but few have survived. The chairs with sunburst motifs are of similar date.
The paintings:
  Lyonel Robert Tollemache (1774–93). Artist unknown.
  Louisa Manners, Countess of Dysart (1745–1840). Artist unknown.
  Lady Frances Tollemache (1738–1807) by Daniel Gardiner (?1750–1805).

MUSEUM ROOM

(*Some visitors may prefer to return to this room after completing the tour of the State Rooms.*)
Formerly a bedroom known as 'The Room over the Chapel', this room has long been set aside for the display of costumes and other rare textiles. It was recently remodelled to enable adequate protection from light, dirt and general wear-and-tear to be given to the contents, including one specimen of each of the remarkable sets of chairs in the house which still retain their original upholstery (pl. 11). This will ensure the survival of at least one example of each type for a long time, while visitors may continue to enjoy the spectacle presented by the rest of this very rare furniture set out in the rooms for which it was designed. Some of the other textile objects belonging to the house are also shown in this room and a case with fragments surviving from the

rich upholstery decoration of the house will, it is hoped, remind the visitor that the sumptuous appearance of this house during the 17th century was largely achieved by means of such rich textiles and by elaborate upholstery which constituted the most striking (and expensive) part of the overall effect.

The long case contains the specimens of upholstered chairs, together with a panel of 'gilt leather' dating from about 1680, which may have come from the Lauderdale's house in Whitehall. There is also a table with rare objects of various kinds, including:

A sermon preached upon the first occasion after the death of his Grace John Duke of Lauderdale in the Chappel at Ham by John Gaskarth, his late Grace's Chaplain. Dated 1683.

A Book of Common Prayer. Dated 1625. Probably given to William Murray, 1st Earl of Dysart, by Charles I.

At the end of the room is a toilet set, comprising a *toilette* or cloth for laying on a dressing-table, a dressing mirror, a comb-case, brushes, boxes, etc., as well as a dressing-gown and pair of mules. The set is made of a rich Lyons silk brocaded with silver and must have been purchased on the occasion of the marriage of the 4th Earl of Dysart to Grace Carteret in 1729. Such sets were not uncommonly given as wedding-presents by those who could afford such

luxuries. It is in a quite remarkable state of preservation.

The original inventory of 1679 can be seen in the small wall-case.

THE CABINET OF MINIATURES

Formerly the Servant's Room for the bedchamber known as the Room over the Chapel, this little room now houses a collection of miniatures. In the 17th century many of these were on open display, together with a number of the smaller oil paintings, on the walls of the Green Closet, where they complemented the collection of large portraits in the adjoining Long Gallery.

The most notable are as follows:

Queen Elizabeth I (1533–1603) by Nicholas Hilliard (1547–1619).

An unknown Man against a Background of Flames (a conceit symbolic of consuming love) by Isaac Oliver (d. 1617).

An unknown Child. Style of Isaac Oliver (d. 1617).

An unknown Lady signed Samuel Cooper (1609–72).

Henry Rich, Earl of Holland (1590–1649). Studio of John Hoskins.

Charles II (1630–85. As a youth) signed David des Granges (c. 1611–c. 1675).

Mary Beatrice D'Este (1658–1718. Wife of James II) signed Lawrence Crosse (d. 1724).

In the same case is a lock of hair said to have been cut from the head of Robert Devereux, Earl of Essex, Queen Elizabeth's favourite, on the morning of his execution, 25 February 1601. The relic belonged to his daughter, Frances, Duchess of Somerset, passed to her grand-daughter, Lady Weymouth, and from the latter to Lady Worsley, who left 'my ruby ring with the lock' to her grand-daughter, Grace, Lady Dysart.

THE ROUND GALLERY

At the time of the Lauderdales this room, which was divided by a floor from the room below, served as the 'Great Dining Room'. It is the first of the series of State Rooms leading up to the Queen's Bedchamber —the culminating room in the sequence of impressive *chambres de parade* created for show or for entertaining important guests. The rooms are now viewed in the sequence planned in the 17th century and the visitor is taken through each room until the Bedchamber is reached. It is only by viewing these ancient houses in the way intended by their builders that one can really hope to obtain a proper understanding of their arrangement—and therefore how they came to be designed as they are.

11. *(left)*
Armchair covered with figured velvet; mid-18th century

29

12. *Duke and Duchess of Lauderdale*
by Sir Peter Lely

The plaster ceiling, (which shows the influence of Inigo Jones) and the frieze were made by Kinsman the plasterer in 1637 or 1638. The principal furniture under the Lauderdales consisted of eight cedar tables, eighteen walnut chairs covered in crimson velvet, some screens and two sideboards (which now stand in the Queen's Bedchamber). The cedar tables were perhaps normally hidden by the screens and only brought out when needed. They could be used separately or put together to form one large table.

It is uncertain exactly when the room was converted into a gallery, but it must have been early in the eighteenth century, since an inventory dated 1727 refers to 'the Hall Gallery' and another inventory, undated but probably made about the same time, calls it 'the Open Room over ye Hall'. Some of the existing balusters, however, are of later date and made of iron.

Inset paintings:

Naked Boys with Lions by Francis Cleyn (1582–1658).

Tobias and the Angel after the painting by Adam Elsheimer (1578 ?–1610) at Frankfurt-am-Main. Probably by an artist of the Antwerp School. About 1640.

Hanging paintings:

Grace Carteret, Countess of Dysart, with a Girl and a Black Servant by John Vanderbank (1694 ?–1739).

Group of Gentlemen on the Grand Tour attributed to Philip Wickstead (active 1763–c. 1790). (The second figure from the left is said to be 'Mr Tollemache'—probably Captain the Honourable John Tollemache, R.N.).

Lieutenant General Thomas Tollemache (c. 1651–94) by Sir Godfrey Kneller (1645–1723).

Frances Worsley, Lady Carteret (1694–1743. Mother of Grace, Countess of Dysart) by Sir Godfrey Kneller. About 1715.

An unknown Youth attributed to Cornelius Johnson.

Daniel in the Lions' Den attributed to Jacopo Bassano (1510–92). Venetian School.

Elizabeth Dysart in Youth by Sir Peter Lely (1618–80). This portrait, one of the most notable in the house, dates from the early fifties. Silvery in tone and romantic in conception, it is yet more interpretative of character than most of Lely's portraits of fashionable ladies, and may certainly be counted among his finest works (pl. 24).

The Passage of the Red Sea signed by Jakob de Wett (1610– after 1671), a pupil of Rembrandt.

Mrs Heneage (Mother of Henrietta Cavendish, Lady Huntingtower) attributed to William Wissing (1656–87).

A portrait of '*Both Ye Graces in one Picture*' (to quote the 1679 inventory) by Lely (pl. 12). Painted in the late seventies, only a few years before the death of the artist, it presents a remarkable contrast to the earlier portrait of the Duchess both in style and characterization. The representation of the Duke recalls Lord Ailesbury's reference to his complexion—'his head was toward that of a Saracen fiery face'!

THE NORTH DRAWING ROOM

(frontispiece)
The plaster frieze and ceiling were made in 1637 by Kinsman, the plasterer who made the ceilings of the Staircase and Round Gallery. His charge for work done in this room was £35 4s.

At the same time, Carter, the joiner employed by William Murray, charged £5 10s for wainscoting in this room and £12 for a pair of doors and door-cases; he also made two picture frames and two windows.

The tapestries were woven of silk and wool by ex-Mortlake weavers, perhaps at Soho. They can be dated between 1699 and 1719 from the arms of Lord (later Earl) Shelburne. The scenes are partly derived from the earlier Mortlake series of 'The Months' (which were themselves derived with modifications from Flemish originals), and are put together in rather arbitrary sequences as follows:

1. Milking: April.

13. Armchair carved with dolphins

2. Ploughing and sowing: September.
3. Sheep-shearing and hay-making: June, July.
4. Hawking and reaping: May, August.
5. Vintage: October.

The gilded chairs, carved with dolphins, (pl. 13) still sport their original silk covers and are thus objects of the very greatest rarity. They are from a set of six armchairs and six 'backstooles' (the name often given to sidechairs at the time) that were listed as being in this room in 1679. Their form is based on contemporary French fashions but the chairs may well have been made in Holland; an English provenance is less likely. One armchair from the set is displayed in the Museum Room (see p. 27).

The cabinet veneered with ivory was also in the room in 1679 and must at the time have been specially prized, if one considers the large quantity of ivory that went into its making. The contemporary Persian carpet on the floor must likewise have been regarded as a very precious object and, in those days, was normally kept rolled up in the Wardrobe Room upstairs.

The carved and gilded candlestands have shafts in the form of twisted columns, entwined with vines; this Baroque form is seen again in the twisted half-columns flanking the fireplace (see below). The brass fire-dogs stood in the adjoining 'Great Dining Room' in the time of the Lauderdales. The four inset pictures are attributed in the 1683 inventory to 'Decline'—a variant of the name of Francis Cleyn (1582–1658), a German artist who after a period of study in Italy entered the service of Christian IV of Denmark and afterwards came to England, where he was appointed designer to the Mortlake tapestry works by James I.[1] Cleyn was the principal decorator in this country at the time and executed many important commissions including painted mural decorations for Carew House and Somerset House, and the designing of the imposing 'Gilt Room' at Holland House, Kensington (destroyed in the last war). The paintings here, done in tempera on paper, were doubtless commissioned by William Murray. They are very dilapidated (the examples of Cleyn's work in the adjoining Green Closet are in far better state), but they possess a certain interest in so far as they associate Cleyn with the room and suggest that he had a hand in designing the striking architectural decoration. It is significant that the twisted half columns flanking the fireplace are copied direct from a work with which Cleyn was very familiar—Raphael's cartoon of the healing of the lame man at the temple gate, part of the famous *Acts of the Apostles*, which were acquired by Charles I and many times served

[1]Among the tapestries he designed the best known is the series representing the story of Hero and Leander, one piece of which is in the Victoria and Albert Museum.

14. Ceiling of the
Green Closet

15. Detail of table in the Green Closet

as a model to the Mortlake weavers.[1] The roundel over the door to the Green Closet is a copy of the head of Helen from Guido Reni's *Rape of Helen* in the Louvre.

THE GREEN CLOSET

This room is a rare survival of a closet from the time of Charles I. The hangings are 19th century replacements but convey the appearance of the room after the re-furnishing of the 1670s. The walls were at that time covered with more than fifty miniatures and small paintings.

The furniture is listed in the 1679 inventory as follows:

One ebony table garnished with silver. In the centre of the top (which has been renewed) the silver plaque bears the initials E. D. for Elizabeth Dysart and a Countess's coronet, suggesting that the table was made before 1672 when she became Duchess of Lauderdale.

Two Japan Cabinets and frames. This pair of Japanese lacquer cabinets dates from the 1630s.

[1]There is a series of large-scale drawings from Raphael's cartoons by Francis Cleyn and his son the younger Francis (?) in the Ashmolean Museum. The cartoons, which are the property of H. M. The Queen, are on loan to the Victoria and Albert Museum.

Two squobb frames, two seats upon them covered with green damask, and green sarsnet cases. This refers to the long stools against the wall; a squab was a heavily stuffed cushion forming a seat. (The seat-rails have been renewed).

In the fireplace is a fender decorated with foliated scrolls in keeping with the carved ornament of the chimney-piece.

The paintings by Francis Cleyn that decorate the cove and ceiling are done in tempera on paper and may well first have served as cartoons for tapestries. The same subjects with the same background occur in two panels of tapestry belonging to a set at Hardwick Hall, Derbyshire, woven at Hatton Garden some twenty years after Cleyn's death. Like the inset paintings in the Marble Dining Room downstairs, they are based on 16th century paintings by Polidoro Caldara.

Hanging paintings:

These include three portraits after Daniel Mytens: *James I* (over fireplace), *James, 2nd Marquess of Hamilton* (left) and *Lodovick Stuart, Duke of Lennox and Richmond* (right). They were re-framed in the 18th century.

The two carved limewood picture frames are characteristic products of the school of carvers who were influenced by Grinling Gibbons in the last quarter of the 17th century.

16. Long
Gallery
(*National Trust*)

THE LONG GALLERY

The Gallery formed part of the original house but was completely redecorated by William Murray in 1639. The work was done by Carter, the joiner, and his bill is still extant:

Item in the Gallerie wainscott that was taken asunder and new made and all the mouldings of the wainscott at 4s the yarde £36. 0. 0
Item for new work with the pedistalls 72 yards at 6s the yarde £21. 12. 0
Item 20 palasters of my one (own) stuff £10. 10. 0

This fine panelling still survives, although it was slightly altered when the new rooms on the South Front were added in the 1670s.

The scanty furniture and the absence of a fireplace indicate that the Gallery here, as in other great houses, was intended for show and exercise rather than comfort. The effect depended chiefly on the array of 'Two & Twenty Pictures with Carvd Guilt Frames'. The bills for the frames, which are all of a set, date from 1672 to 1675 and show that they cost 70s each.

The furniture is listed in the 1679 inventory as follows:

One black ebony Cabinet and frame. This is still here.

Four Squobbs with Cases of purple and white Sarsnet. These four seats have vestiges of japanned decoration on their bulbous legs. Their modern covers of hand-woven Indian cotton seek to reproduce the general appearance of their original covers of purple and white checked Indian taffeta.

One Indian Cabinet with a gilt frame carved. This refers to the handsome Japanese lacquer cabinet, the stand of which may well have been made by Dutch craftsmen (pl. 17).

Two arme Chayres, carved frames, of walnut tree. Probably the pair that are here now (pl. 18), the gilding having been added later. They were re-upholstered in the 1960s.

Seavon boxes carv'd & guilt for tuby roses. Six of these still survive.

One table and stands of Inlaid marble. Described in an earlier inventory as being of 'counterfeit marble'. The table has not survived but the octagonal tops of the present 18th century candlestands are of scagliola, or imitation marble, and presumably survive from the 17th century originals.

Two great Globes and two small Globes. A terrestrial and a celestial globe survive, with their original protective leather covers.

The curtains are modern reproductions, based on the descriptions of those that hung here in the 17th century.

The paintings:

William, 2nd Duke of Hamilton (1616–57) attributed to Cornelius Johnson.

17. Japanese lacquer cabinet

Self-portrait after Van Dyck. The artist is shown pointing to a sunflower with one hand, while with the other he displays the gold chain bestowed on him by Charles I, apparently identifying himself with the sunflower and thus illustrating allegorically his devotion to the King.[1] Several versions exist.

Called the *Countess of Southampton*. Artist unknown.

Lucy, Countess of Carlisle (1599–1660). Celebrated for her beauty and political intrigues. During the Commonwealth she was a neighbour of Lady Dysart at Petersham, where according to a contemporary 'she enjoyed herself more in this Retiredness than in all her former Vanities'.[2] After Van Dyck.

Called *Ann, Countess of Bedford* (d. 1684) by Sir Peter Lely.

Duchess of Lauderdale with a Black Servant by Sir Peter Lely.

Lady Maynard (d. 1682. The Duchess's youngest sister) by Sir Peter Lely.

Catherine Bruce, Countess of Dysart (d. 1649. The Duchess's mother). Artist unknown.

[1] See the article on this portrait by R. R. Wark in the *Burlington Magazine*, February 1956, pp. 53–4.

[2] From a letter of Brian Duppa, afterwards Bishop of Winchester, in the possession of Sir Giles Isham, Bt.

18. Armchair of walnut, partly gilded

Elizabeth Tollemache, Duchess of Argyll (d. 1735. The Duchess's elder daughter) by Sir Peter Lely.
Lady Doune (the Duchess's younger daughter). Artist unknown.

William Murray, Earl of Dysart (d. 1655. The Duchess's father) by Cornelius Johnson. Murray also figures in a well-known picture by William Dobson in the collection of Lord Sandys, where he is shown with Prince Rupert persuading Colonel John Russell (see portrait at the other end of Gallery), who had given up his commission, to re-join the Royalist forces.

Sir John Maitland, 1st Baron Maitland of Thirlestane (1545?–1595. Lord Chancellor of Scotland; grandfather of the Duke of Lauderdale). Artist unknown.

Charles I (1600–49). Studio of Van Dyck. There are several versions. This one was probably given to William Murray by the king, as indicated by a note in a Memorandum of pictures bought by the king from Van Dyck, dated 1638–39, which reads 'le Roi vestu de noir a Monr Morre' (doubtless a French variant of Murray).

?Sir Henry Vane, the Younger (b. 1613; executed 1662. A leading parliamentarian under the Commonwealth) by Sir Peter Lely.

?William, Lord Alington (1610–48. First husband of Elizabeth Tollemache, sister of Sir Lyonel

39

Tollemache, the Duchess's first husband) by Sir Peter Lely.

?Sir Charles Compton (d. 1661. A prominent Cavalier leader) by Sir Peter Lely.

The Duke of Lauderdale in Garter Robes. School of Lely.

Charles II. School of Lely.

Thomas Clifford, 1st Baron Clifford of Chudleigh (1630–73. Lord Treasurer 1672. A member of the 'Cabal') after Lely. Versions by the artist are at Ugbrooke and Cirencester Park.[1]

Traditionally called *Lyonel Tollemache, 3rd Earl of Dysart* (1648–1726. The Duchess of Lauderdale's eldest son) by Sir Peter Lely. The sitter is now thought, however, to be John Leslie, 7th Earl and 1st Duke of Rothes (d. 1681), who became Chancellor of Scotland.

Sir William Compton (d. 1663. Brother of Sir Charles and like him a distinguished Cavalier commander. He was the second husband of Elizabeth, sister of Sir Lyonel Tollemache, 3rd Bt, the Duchess's first husband) by Sir Peter Lely. There is another version in the National Portrait Gallery.

Colonel John Russell (one of Charles I's officers in the Civil War. After the Restoration first colonel of the First Foot, now Grenadier Guards) by

[1] See *Catalogue of Bathurst portraits*, pp. 42–8.

John Michael Wright (1617–?1700). Signed and dated 1659. A Scot by birth, Wright was one of the few native artists of real individuality and technical accomplishment among the host of foreign portrait painters who practised in England under the Stuarts. It is an early and very attractive portrait by a painter whose output was relatively small.

THE LIBRARY

The Library and its anteroom (or 'Closet' as it was called) were among the rooms added to the house by the Duke and Duchess of Lauderdale. The change of style is clearly seen in the ceiling, which, instead of being divided into compartments by heavy bands of plasterwork, as in the State Apartments on the north side, is lightly ornamented with a wreath of laurels in the centre and in the corners with four panels filled with graceful foliated sprays. The plasterer, Henry Wells, in his bill dated 1674 charged for '25 yards of frettwork in ye library at six shill. six pence ye yard'.

Henry Harlow, the joiner, supplied not only such things as the bookshelves and window and door frames but also 'the seder table with drawers In My Lords Librarie' at a cost of £12.

Though unusually small, the Library once contained many rare books, including some works printed by Caxton and Wynkyn de Worde. These have been dispersed. The steps date from about 1740.

In the Library Closet are shown some inset paintings by Bega, taken from rooms to which the public are not admitted.

ANTECHAMBER TO THE QUEEN'S BEDCHAMBER

This room was known as the Green Drawing Room in 1679, when the walls were hung with green silk and velvet. By 1683 the present hangings had been installed and it was then designated *The Anti-roome to ye Queen's Chamber*, a name expressive of its function in the formal sequence of State Rooms. Like the Library, it was one of the rooms added by the Lauderdales and has a ceiling of similar type.

The artificially grained wainscoting, the carved swags of fruit and flowers about the chimney-piece and the simple marble moulding that frames the fireplace are typical of the house and of the period. The wall hangings, framed with blue velvet decorated with *appliqué* embroidery, were described in 1683 as having panels of 'blew Damusk' but this has faded to a yellowish brown.

The room contains, as it did in the 17th century, a representative collection of the lacquered and japanned furniture fashionable in the reign of Charles II.

Lacquer had been imported from the East since the reign of Queen Elizabeth I. After the Restoration the demand for it became so strong in England (as well as on the Continent) that the Eastern products were soon imitated on a large scale; but the methods employed were quite different, and are more properly described by the contemporary term 'japanning'. In this room there are both English and Oriental examples. The mirror frame is composed of incised Oriental lacquer cut into panels, regardless of the fact that some of the horsemen and trees are thereby made to appear the wrong way up.[1] The matching table and the cabinet on the elaborately carved and gilded stand have been similarly decorated with strips of lacquer. The candlestands retain their original 17th century lacquer tops *en suite* but the bases have been renewed at a later date. The incised lacquer screens are entirely Oriental. The japanned chairs are survivors from separate but similar sets, some of which are to be seen in the White Closet and the Duchess's Private Closet. In the corner is a japanned

[1] Stalker and Parker, the authors of a *Treatise* on japanning, published in 1688, remark that Bantamwork, as it was called, was out of fashion and that 'no one gives it house-room, except some who have made new Cabinets out of old Skreens'. They criticize the haphazard methods employed in the construction of such furniture, where 'you may observe the finest hodgpodg and medly of Men and Trees turned topsie turvie'.

close-stool, which was kept behind the concealed door in the 17th century. The miniature cabinet is Chinese, its small gilded stand having been added later.

Inset paintings:

Landscape with a Man leading an Ass (over the fireplace); *A Lion Hunt* and *A Landscape with Ruins* (over the doors). All by Dirck van den Bergen.

THE QUEEN'S BEDCHAMBER

From this room one may look out across the garden and down the avenue of trees that stretches out to Ham Common. One then becomes aware that the grounds are disposed symmetrically around an axis which passes straight through the centre of this room, stressing its importance as the culminating room in the sequence of State Rooms on this *piano nobile*. The room was prepared for a visit by Charles II's queen, Catherine of Braganza, but was so much altered in the 18th century that its original purpose can no longer be readily appreciated. However, a model of the room as it must have looked around 1680 is to be seen just outside the Demonstration Room downstairs.

The Queen's bed stood on a raised *parquet* (which was hived off from the rest of the room by a carved balustrade) at the far end of the room, facing the oncoming visitor. Inlaid into the parquetry, on either side of where the bed stood, are the ciphers of the Lauderdales. Made by Henry Harlow at a cost of 35s a square yard, the parquet was described as 'Cedar inlaid wth wallnutt tree'. It was lowered to the level of the rest of the floor when the room was converted into a drawing room but the raised foot-walk (which is necessary to protect it) does suggest the higher level, which continued into the next room. In the time of the Lauderdales there were 'Two leather Covers for the stepp', as we know from the inventories of the period. It was perhaps in honour of Catherine of Braganza that there was a 'Portugall bedstead' in the room, according to the 1679 inventory; this was replaced in winter by one with hangings of blue velvet brocaded with gold. In 1679 a separate set of wall- and bed-hangings was reserved for use in summer, together with a set of 12 chairs to match.

The 1673 bill from the carver, John Bullimore, gives a detailed account, listing each section of the decorative woodwork. For the '6 festons and a crown over ye chimney' he charged £6 10s. The gilding of the same festoons and coronet by Nicholas Moore cost £5 10s.

The plasterwork on the ceiling is similar to that in the last room but here the treatment of the floral scrolls in the spandrels is more accomplished; note

20. Queen's
Bedchamber

21. Gilded chair
in the Queen's
Bedchamber; about
1740

the lively figures of men and animals among the foliage.

The Queen's Bedchamber must have been converted into a drawing room in about 1740, by the 4th Earl of Dysart. This is the approximate date of the tapestries, which are woven with silk and wool and signed by Bradshaw, the English weaver whose work for Holkham, Norfolk (including a set with subjects similar to these), can be dated between 1730 and 1750. The subjects are made up from figures and motifs taken from pictures by Watteau and Pater. The individual hangings are:

1. The Dance.
2. The Fountain.
3. The Swing.
4. The Fruit-gatherer.

The chairs and sofas (pl. 21), the pier-glasses and the console tables all date from about 1740. The walnut tables are the pair of sideboards that stood in the Great Dining Room until it was converted into the Round Gallery; their caryatid supports are an unusual feature and may well be the work of Dutch craftsmen. Also in the Great Dining Room were the Italian candlestands, described in the 1679 inventory as 'Two Blackamore Stands'. The pair of bronzed plaster figures represent Spencer and Milton and were made at the Hyde Park Corner workshop of John Cheere.

The bellows (pl. 22) are overlaid with embossed

45

and chased silver on one side and decorated with marquetry on the other. The shovel, tongs and fire-pan are all mounted with embossed silver, the latter incorporating the Duchess's cypher amid scrolling foliage.

Inset paintings:

The Virgin and Child with St John after Andrea del Sarto (1486–1530). This is a copy of the once famous Pinti Madonna, which has itself been destroyed. *A Landscape* and *A Pair of Lions with a Leopard in a Den* by Dirck van den Bergen.

QUEEN'S CLOSET

This was an entirely private room beyond the Queen's Bedchamber, to which only the most intimate friends of the Queen or the Lauderdales would have been admitted. In order to try and recapture the withdrawn character of this small chamber the public no longer passes through it but may approach and look into it—after which, having seen its riches, they are asked to return along the route by which they came. Even the most august visitor in the 17th century would have followed this procedure.

The ceiling is a smaller version of those in the Queen's Bedchamber and its Antechamber; but here the flat surfaces are painted in imitation of marble and the details of the plaster relief are picked out in gold. The oval panel within the laurel wreath is

22. Bellows, mounted with embossed silver

23. (*right*) Queen's Closet

painted to represent Ganymede and the Eagle and has been attributed to Antonio Verrio.

As in the Queen's Bedchamber, the carver's bill itemises all the decorative details, including '1 sheild' costing £1 and '1 cherubims face', costing 10s.

The original hangings of a brocaded satin with striped silk borders are extremely rare survivals of the most luxurious form of wall-decoration of the period and have recently been restored. They are described as being of 'crimson and gold stuff, bordered with green, gold and silver stuff'.

The panels surrounding the fireplace and on the window sill are of imitation marble (scagliola) and are perhaps the earliest example of this form of decoration in England. The initials 'J. E. L.' (for John and Elizabeth Lauderdale), together with a ducal coronet, are incorporated in the design. The same initials can be seen in the marquetry floor, which originally continued without a break from the raised area in the Queen's Bedchamber.

The armchair, covered in its original silk *en suite* with the wall-hangings, is one of a pair mentioned in the 1679 inventory as having been in this room and described as '2 sleeping chayres, carv'd and guilt frames, covered with crimson and gould stuff with gould fringe'. (The other is now shown in the Museum Room). Note the feet carved as sea-horses and the gilded ratchets for adjusting the angle of the back. Such chairs have become extremely rare but the Duke possessed others and several supplied to Charles II are mentioned in the Royal accounts of the day. The pair of stools are probably the 'Two small squob frames carv'd & guilt' that were in the adjoining Bedchamber in the 17th century. They were each supplied with two cushions. (The present cushions are modern). The small Chinese screen is perhaps the one that was listed as being here in 1679.

The silver-mounted chimney-furniture is contemporary with the rest of the room.

Inset paintings:

Two *Views of Naples* and *A Seaport*, described in the 1683 inventory as 'Three fixt pictures of old Wick' (Thomas Wyck, 1616–77).

Hanging paintings:

Queen Henrietta Maria (1609–69. Queen consort of Charles I) after Van Dyck. This painting formed part of the summer furnishings of the Queen's Bedchamber in 1679.

The visitor should now return through the sequence of State Rooms, just as a visitor viewing this splendid apartment would have done in the 17th century.

HISTORY OF HAM HOUSE

The original Ham House was built in 1610 by Sir Thomas Vavasour, Knight Marshal to James I. A few years later it passed into the possession of a favourite of the King, John Ramsay, Earl of Holderness, who is remembered for the part he played in rescuing the King at the time of the Gowrie conspiracy (1600). Some time after his death (1626) it became the residence and eventually, in 1637, the property of William Murray, first Earl of Dysart, who had served in his youth as 'whipping boy' to the Prince of Wales, later Charles I. This post imposed on him the duty of being whipped for the Prince's misdemeanours; on the other hand it gave him the opportunity, which he did not neglect, of cultivating the friendship of the heir to the throne, and eventually brought him, among other benefits, a peerage and the lease of the manors of Ham and Petersham. Bishop Burnet (in the *History of his own time, 1715*) will have it that he owed his advancement to a gift for intrigue amounting to duplicity, 'being very insinuating, but very false, and of so revengeful a character that rather than any of the counsels given by his enemies should succeed he would have revealed them and betrayed both the King and them. It was generally believed that he had betrayed the most important of all his [the King's] secrets to his enemies.' Burnet adds that 'he had one particular quality, that when he was drunk, which was very often, he was upon a most exact reserve, though he was pretty open at all other times.' However this may be, he had a lively interest in the Arts and was a member of the 'Whitehall group' of collectors and connoisseurs. His advanced taste is shown by the architectual alterations he made at Ham and there is evidence that his house was luxuriously appointed; some of the best paintings in the Ham collection date from his time. He died without a male heir soon after the middle of the century, and was succeeded by his daughter, Elizabeth, who not only became mistress of Ham House, but also contrived (after the Restoration) to obtain the title of Countess of Dysart in her own right, with the power of appointing her successor from among her children.

THE DUKE AND DUCHESS OF LAUDERDALE

Some years before her father's death, probably in 1647, Lady Dysart had married Sir Lyonel Tollemache, 3rd Baronet, of Helmingham Hall in Suffolk.

Sir Lyonel thus became the founder of the long line of Tollemaches who, as Earls of Dysart, succeeded one another at Ham for nearly three hundred years. But he lacked the ruthless ambition which his wife expected of her husband, and long before his death, which occurred in 1669, Lady Dysart had formed a close friendship with the Earl of Lauderdale, a man whose ability and thirst for power made him a more suitable partner for a woman of her calibre. After her husband's death, Lady Dysart had to wait two more years before Lady Lauderdale died; then she promptly married the widower (17 February 1672). In the words of Sir George Mackenzie, a contemporary historian, 'Lady Dysart had such an ascendant over his [Lord Lauderdale's] affections that neither her age, nor his affairs, nor yet the clamour of his friends and the people, more urgent than both of these, could divert him from marrying her within six weeks of his Lady's decease.'

The same writer asserts that Lauderdale 'really yielded to his gratitude, she having formerly saved his life by her mediation with the Usurper' (Oliver Cromwell). There was indeed a fairly general belief among her contemporaries that she had been Cromwell's mistress. According to Burnet, 'Cromwell was certainly fond of her, and she took care to entertain him in it, till he, finding what was said upon it, broke it off.' Under the Commonwealth she was widely reputed to have powerful influence with the Protector; thus, when Sir Justinian Isham was arrested and imprisoned in 1655, his friend Brian Duppa, afterwards Bishop of Winchester, who was at that time a neighbour of Elizabeth Dysart, wrote to him suggesting that she might, if she would, hasten his release.[1] She did much to help the royalist cause and was associated with the Sealed Knot, the secret society that worked for the King's restoration.

Contemporary chroniclers testify to the charms she possessed as a young woman, An early glimpse of her as a girl, long before she met the Duke, is given by Henry Knyvet in a letter to his wife dated 23 May 1644.[2] He declares he has 'growne very well acquainted with the Murryes' and goes on to say that 'the eldest daughter is the jewel, and indeed a pretty one but for her deep coullerd hayer. I knowe not how such a notion would relish, but 'tis sayd she is like to be a very great fortune . . . Indeed, sweet Hart, such a pretty witty lass, with such a brave house and state as she is like to have, m'thinks might make a

[1]'I am still of the Mind, that your Restraint will not be long; but probably some means must first be used. What think you, if I should repair to the good Lady in my Neighbourhood, who was wont to have a great deal of kindness for you?' From a letter in the possession of Sir Giles Isham, Bt. It is clear from the previous correspondence that Elizabeth Dysart is the lady referred to.

[2]B. Schofield, ed., *The Knyvet letters*, 1949, pp. 151–2.

24. *(left)*
Duchess of
Lauderdale in
her Youth by Sir
Peter Lely

25. *(right)*
Duke of
Lauderdale by
Edmund Ashfield

young fellow think her hayer very beautifull. I could find in my hart to wooe her for my sonne, for I am much in her favore. She seems to be a very good harmless vertuouse witty little bable.'

The captivating portrait by Lely (pl. 24) in the Round Gallery was painted only a few years after these words were written and bears out Knyvet's account, save for the 'deep coullerd' hair. Another portrait by Lely in the same gallery reveals her in middle age, seated beside her second husband the Duke (as he had by then become). She had been deeply involved in politics and court intrigues during particularly troubled times and she had made many enemies. Bishop Burnet summarized her character thus: 'She was a woman of great beauty', he wrote, 'but of far greater parts; had a wonderful quickness of apprehension, and an amazing vivacity in conversation; had studied not only divinity and history, but mathematics and philosophy; but what ruined these accomplishments, she was restless in her ambition, profuse in her expense, and of a most ravenous covetousness; nor was there anything she stuck at to compass her end, for she was violent in everything—a violent friend, and a much more violent enemy.' Yet the concern she showed for her children's welfare and her kindness to friends in trouble are evidence that she also had a gentler side to her character. In the furnishing of her remodelled house she showed considerable taste and it may be that she sought advice in these matters from her cousin, the eminent Scottish architect, Sir William Bruce.

Her second husband, John Maitland, afterwards Duke of Lauderdale, was born in 1616, and began his career as a leader of the Scottish Covenanters; but towards the end of the Civil War, having formed a firm and lasting friendship with the future Charles II, he abandoned that cause and went over to the Royalists. He was with Charles at the Battle of Worcester, where, less fortunate than his master, he was captured by the Parliamentarians, who held him prisoner until the Restoration.

When free again, Lauderdale quickly re-established his former influence over the King, and obtained the appointment of Secretary for Scotland, a post which he held for the next twenty years. Among the several ministries of which he was a member was the notorious 'Cabal', so called because the initials of the five trusted ministers who dominated it spelt the word CABAL.[1] The Queen's Bedchamber is popularly known as the 'Cabal Room', but the celebrated Cabal could not have met there, as the ministry had been dissolved before the room was completed.

[1]Cabal, i.e. clique, coterie, faction. The members were Clifford, Ashley, Buckingham, Arlington and Lauderdale. Of the latter Macaulay writes: 'loud and coarse both in mirth and anger, (he) was perhaps, under his outward show of boisterous frankness, the most dishonest man in the whole Cabal.'

Lauderdale's position was particularly strong, since no other minister was concerned with Scotland; and Charles was usually quite ready to allow him a free hand in that country, provided he supported the King's personal policy in English and foreign affairs. At first conciliatory, Lauderdale's Scottish policy afterwards became increasingly severe, and ruthless measures were employed against his former friends the Covenanters. Some said the change from leniency became particularly marked in 1672 after his marriage with Lady Dysart. The no doubt biassed Bishop Burnet wrote that 'The Earl of Lauderdale had acted with much steadiness and uniformity before, but at this time there happened a great alteration in his temper, occasioned by the humours of a profuse, imperious woman . . . After her husband's death she became so intimate with him, and gained such an ascendant over him, as much lessened him in the opinion of the world. For all applications were made to her; she sold places and disposed of offices, and took upon her not only to determine everything of this nature, but to direct his private conduct likewise, and as conceit took her would make him fall out with all his friends.' Yet a contributory cause of Lauderdale's harshness was undoubtedly his deteriorating health, with much pain from a kidney disease. He had, too, the difficult task of carrying out the King's policies against constant opposition from a great number of his countrymen.

Lauderdale was created a Duke in 1672. That year probably marked the zenith of his fortunes, for, although he remained entrenched in office for eight more years, his conduct of affairs thenceforward aroused strong opposition in England as well as in Scotland; he was violently assailed in the House of Commons and only the King's favour, which he never lost, maintained him in power. By 1680 his health had begun to fail and he was forced to resign. Two years later he died, his Duchess surviving him until 1698. His aspect, character and versatile temperament are described by Burnet, who knew him well, in a passage so full of colour and detail that it may be quoted in full: 'In his person he made but an ill appearance. His stature was large, his hair red, his tongue too big for his mouth, and his whole manner rough and boisterous, and very unfit for a Court. His temper was intolerable, for he was haughty beyond expression to all who had expectances from him, but abject where himself had any; and so violently passionate that he oftentimes, upon slight occasions, ran himself into fits like madness. His learning was considerable, for he not only understood Latin, in which he was a master, but Greek and Hebrew; had read a great deal of divinity, almost all historians both ancient and modern; and having besides an extraordinary memory, was furnished with a copious but very unpolished way of expression. The sense of religion that a long imprisonment had

impressed on his mind was soon erased by a course of luxury and sensuality, which ran him into great expense, and which he stuck at nothing to support; and the fury of his behaviour heightened the severity of his ministry, and made it more like the cruelty of an Inquisition than the legality of justice . . . He was the coldest friend and the most violent enemy that ever was known'—a cruel summary of his character by a hostile witness.

As for Burnet's strictures on his manners at court, a contemporary has left a curious account of them. He relates that Lauderdale was ever 'uttering bald jests for wit, and repeating good ones of others, and ever spoiled them in relating them, which delighted the good King much . . . Besides tiring the King with his bald jests, he was continually putting his fingers into the King's snuff-box, which obliged him to order one to be made which he wore with a string on his wrist, and did not open, but the snuff came out by shaking. The King did some of his court honour to dine or sup with them, and a select company, agreeable to his pleasant and witty humour. This Lord although not invited ever intruded himself.'[1] Yet other accounts suggest that he knew how on occasion to divert the King. James Kirkton, a Scottish historian, who accuses the Duke of having been the King's 'privado in his secret pleasures',

[1] Thomas Bruce, 2nd Earl of Ailesbury, *Memoirs*, Roxburgh Club, 1890.

relates the improbable story that after the destruction of the fleet by the Dutch in the Medway, 'he [Lauderdale] came to the privy chamber and danced in a petticoat to dispell the King's melancholly.'[1]

HAM IN THE SEVENTEENTH CENTURY

By her marriage with the Duke of Lauderdale in 1672, Elizabeth Dysart had become a power in the State and bore herself accordingly. Burnet records that 'they lived at a vast rate, but she set everything to sale to raise money, carrying herself with a haughtiness that would have been shocking in a queen.' Ham House, where they took up residence, soon proved too small, and extensive alterations were undertaken. The building accounts show that the work was begun in 1672 and completed in the winter of 1674–5.

The original Ham House, as we have seen, had been built in 1610 by Sir Thomas Vavasour, a soldier and courtier, whose initials together with the date and the words 'VIVAT REX' are carved on the north door. There is a contemporary plan of the house and gardens among the collection of drawings by Robert Smythson, the Jacobean architect, at the Royal Institute of British Architects (pl. 26). It shows that like many houses of the period, Sir Thomas's home was planned in the form of an H, with a large hall in the centre and a staircase at one end. It is clear from Smythson's drawing that the whole northern section of the house, including the two loggias and the forecourt, still conforms to the original plan, despite certain later alterations to the façade.

Before the house became the property of Elizabeth Dysart, the interior had already been considerably altered by her father, William Murray. The bills of some of the craftsmen show that the work was begun in 1637, the year in which Murray took over the lease. Much of it still survives, including the wainscoting in the Long Gallery and the ornamented plaster ceilings over the Staircase, the Round Gallery and the North Drawing Room. A reference in these bills to the 'new great staires' also proves that the existing staircase was constructed at the same date. Murray's widow made the house over to her daughter and the latter no doubt made a number of changes during the 1650s and 1660s before she married Lauderdale in 1672.

It is probable that a certain amount of furniture was acquired for the house in the 1660s—notably

[1] J. Kirkton, *The secret and true history of the church of Scotland, etc.*, written before 1699, published 1817.

26. (*right*)
Robert Smythson's plan showing the lay-out of the house and grounds in about 1610

27. (*far right*)
Plan of the house and grounds in about 1671. Attributed to John Slezer and Jan Wyck

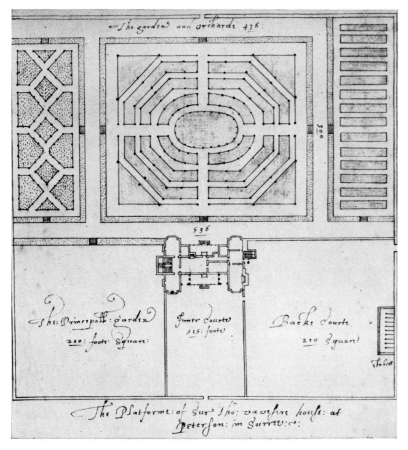

The garden and orchardi 436

300

436

The: Principall: garden
210: foote: Square:

Inner Courte
115: foote

Backe Courte
210: Square)

The Platforme: of Sur: Tho: vachers house: at
Peterson: in Surrie:

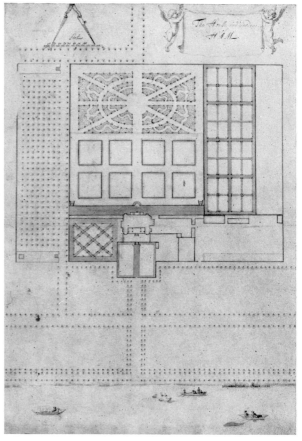

The Hall at Richmont
H: M:

the ebony table with silver mounts bearing Elizabeth Dysart's initials but probably also the pair of walnut sideboards with caryatids.

The architect consulted when Elizabeth Dysart decided to enlarge her house was her cousin, Sir William Bruce, soon to become Surveyor-General of the Royal Works in Scotland. It was decided to almost double the accommodation by building a new series of rooms between the wings on the South Front and a small extension at either end. The proposals are illustrated in two watercolour drawings at the house dating from about 1671. One (pl. 27) is a plan of the house and gardens, the other (pl. 30) shows the South Front as it was to be remodelled. They are attributed to John Slezer, a German engineer and surveyor who was also employed by Lauderdale at Thirlestane Castle, and the Dutch artist, Jan Wyck, one of whose paintings is in the Duke's Dressing Room. The work was in fact carried out by the gentleman architect William Samwell (1628–76) between 1672 and 1674, with only minor alterations to the original proposals (see pl. 31).

The painting in the White Closet (front cover) shows the South Front soon after the completion of the work. Although sash windows were fitted in the new rooms they were probably made to resemble the Jacobean ones, with their old-fashioned mullions and transoms, which were retained at the ends of the wings. An early 18th century writer, praising the

28. The North Front before the Lauderdales altered it. (Detail from a miniature by Alexander Marshall)

29. The North Front today

56

30. Perspective view of the South Front, showing the 'Wilderness'. About 1671

alterations at Ham, makes this interesting comment on the retention of the bay window, a feature that had long been out of fashion: 'The deformity (as now it is esteem'd) of Compass windows, is so disguised either with ye furniture within wch reduceth all to a square, or els by birdcages, and such Conceits without . . . that it appears to No offence.'[1] Since then the south front has undergone various changes; the Jacobean bays have been rebuilt in a later style and on a larger scale, with balconies and Venetian windows above, while all the old window-frames have been replaced with sashes of the familiar type. Moreover, the ancient stonework, including the quoins and the cornice, has been refaced with cement.

On the north side the Lauderdales made no additions but carried out important alterations to the façade. The appearance of the house on that side shortly before they touched it can be gathered from a miniature painting (present whereabouts unknown) by Alexander Marshall, a rare and little-known artist active during the reign of Charles II. It is a version of Hoskins's portrait miniature (at the house) of Catherine Murray, the Duchess's mother, but differs from the original in that it has a view of Ham in the background (pl. 28). The most conspicuous feature of the house, as here represented, is a pair of turrets rising above the roof immediately over the two loggias. The Duke and Duchess removed these turrets and continued the line of the roof at an even level all round the building. Furthermore, they inserted above the ground-floor windows and in the walls of the forecourt a row of niches, in which they placed, according to the 1679 inventory, 'six marble heads and 38 heads of lead'. (The 38 lead busts are still there, though they are surfaced to look like stone; there are also three plaster busts in the 'Cloisters' and a stone one over the front door). Thus modified, the north façade must have looked much as it does today (pl. 29). But Marshall's miniature reveals several interesting differences in the approaches to the house. A straight canal bordered with trees apparently led direct from the Thames to a water-gate in the centre of the wall that then closed the fourth side of the forecourt. Canal, avenue, water-gate and the wall across the front of the courtyard have been swept away. The present gravel terrace with its railings must have been created in 1799–1800 (the dates on the pineapples) but the gate piers surmounted by urns date from about 1671, though subsequently moved further away from the house. The wrought-iron gates (objects of great rarity) are probably those supplied in the same year. They were recorded as having been painted 'small blew' and gilded. The large figure of a river-god in the middle of the forecourt and the pineapples are of

[1] British Museum, *Roger North Works, vol. xiii.*

HAM HOUSE   IN SURREY

'Coade' stone, an artificial composition which had been invented in 1769 and was much used in the late 18th century for architectural ornaments. Coade's catalogue of 1784 advertises 'A River God, 9 feet high, with an Urn through which a stream of water may be carried (100 gns).'

The gardens in the time of the Lauderdales possessed an extraordinary prestige. John Evelyn, who was accustomed to grandeur, was delighted with a visit which he made in 1678. 'After dinner I walked to Ham', he wrote in his diary, 'to see the House and Garden of the Duke of Lauderdale, which is indeed inferior to few of the best Villas in Italy itself; the House furnished like a great Prince's; the Parterres, Flower Gardens, Orangeries, Groves, Avenues, Courts, Statues, Perspectives, Fountains, Aviaries, & all this at the banks of the Sweetest River in the World, must needs be surprising.'

A vivid impression of the house and grounds as they must have appeared to Evelyn is conveyed by the contemporary oil painting of the south front (front cover). It is in a style reminiscent of the 'views' attributed (often on slender evidence) to the immigrant Dutch artist Henry Danckerts, and shows a fashionable party assembled in the garden. The Duke can be recognized in the centre from the Garter Star on his breast; he advances towards his guests with the Duchess on his arm, while an obsequious servant bows to the ground; the black-clothed figure following modestly behind no doubt represents Dr John Gaskarth, the Duke's domestic chaplain, whose adulatory funeral sermon pronounced a few years later on his dead master may still be read in the Museum Room.

The gardens seem to have been little changed by 1739, when the bird's-eye view (pl. 32) was published (in a now rare edition of *Vitruvius Britannicus*), except for the disappearance of the statues and of the seats with cockleshell backs (similar to those believed to have been designed by Francis Cleyn for Holland House, of which there is an example in the Victoria and Albert Museum). Some time later, however, the gravel paths were removed to create an enormous lawn, rhododendrons and other inappropriate species were introduced and the Wilderness was allowed to become very overgrown. In 1975, as a contribution to European Architectural Heritage Year, the National Trust decided to restore the gardens to their late 17th century appearance. The Wilderness has now been cleared and replanted (the old paths had never completely disappeared) and the turf is once again divided by broad gravel walks into eight square plats.

It was on the interior of the building, above all on the new apartments on the south side, that the Lauderdales lavished their substance. The rooms are surprisingly small, considering the rank of the owners; but the Duke and Duchess were evidently

31. (*left*)
Architect's drawing of the South Front. Attributed to William Samwell

61

32. Bird's-eye view of the house and grounds. From an engraving published in *Vitruvius Britannicus* in 1739

determined to make up for lack of space by profusion of ornament. In this they succeeded so well that some of the smallest rooms give the impression of being the most sumptuous. The ceilings, the woodwork, the hangings, the chimney-pieces, the furniture, the elaborate parquetry floors and the silvermounted chimney-furniture were designed and executed with meticulous attention to detail and a careful regard to the total effect.

In 1677, soon after the tasks of decorating and furnishing had been completed, an inventory of the contents was made; another was taken in 1679 and a third in 1683, a year after the Duke's death. Much of the furniture in the house today, and many of the paintings, can be recognized in these interesting documents, as we have already shown. They are detailed enough to give us a clear idea of the former appearance of each room and enable us to furnish most of them as they were in the time of the Lauderdales; they bear out Evelyn's observation that the house was 'furnished like a great Prince's' and show that it was above all rich in hangings and upholstery. In all the principal rooms, including the bedchambers, the walls were hung with tapestry, damask, velvet or mohair, suitably trimmed, with window curtains designed to match or to form a contrast; the numerous bedsteads were also hung with sumptuous materials, and in many cases the chairs were upholstered in the same stuff. This riot of colours must have created an effect of uncommon splendour; a faint conception of it may still be obtained from the existing wall-hangings and tapestries and from the upholstery of the chairs (including the specimens now displayed in the special Museum Room), though time has dulled their once bright hues. Indeed, in original hangings and upholstery, Ham is probably richer than any other contemporary house.

The builder in charge under William Samwell was Arthur Forbes. Most of the joinery seems to have been done by Henry Harlow, who also made furniture and fittings for the Chapel and Library. John Bullimore was responsible for the decorative carving, while the painting and gilding were carried out by Nicholas Moore. There is a bill for the plasterwork in the Library from Henry Wells and there is little doubt that he was also responsible for the ceilings of the Queen's Bedchamber and Closet and the Antechamber. The bills of Augustine Beare, the glazier, show that the new sashes were fitted with 60 panes to a window, just like the existing casements, which they no doubt resembled (see the painting of the South Front, reproduced on the front cover). It is particularly interesting to learn that double glazing was installed in each of the small closets at the ends of the South Front. Also employed were Thomas Turner and William Smith (bricklayers), John Lampen (mason), Thomas Gally (joiner) and

Humphrey Owen (carpenter).

It seems that some of the decorative work was carried out by foreign, notably Dutch, artists and craftsmen. It is clear from Lauderdale's correspondence that Dutch joiners and carvers were employed about the house. For instance, in a letter dated 15 April 1673, he mentions two excellent 'German' joiners who, he says, 'have wrought much for the finishing of this house, and have made the double chassees[1] for the windows; in a word they are sober fellows, understand English enough, and most excellent workmen, both at that trade and for making cabinets.' The Duke had no doubt confused German and Dutch, for in another letter written the same year he again praises 'the two Dutchmen, who are excellent joiners' and 'who made the shapies and lyneings of my rooms at Ham.' Obviously much of the furniture must have been made in this country but we know that some came from Holland and many of the present pieces are very Dutch in character. However, some of the furniture at Ham is of such high quality that it seems unlikely that it can have been made at the house by the craftsmen employed to make sash windows. As a great many Dutch craftsmen were working in London at the time, it is more likely that the finest furniture in the house was made in the metropolis, perhaps even by the same cabinetmakers and upholsterers who produced furniture for the King. On the other hand, the Duke of Lauderdale wrote to Sir William Bruce in 1671 that, 'I like very well the way you have taken to bring those things for me from Holland', so it is also possible that some of the Ham furniture was imported from the Netherlands. Whatever the case may be, the Dutch influence is very strong.

The decorative paintings were likewise commissioned from foreign artists. Ham House contains one of the finest collections of these inset paintings, which were an important feature in the interior design of Restoration houses. The ceiling in the White Closet can be confidently assigned to Antonio Verrio (1639 ?–1707), the Italian artist, who enjoyed a wide patronage in England and was employed at Windsor Castle by Charles II and James II and at Hampton Court Palace by William III and Mary. But most of the numerous inset pictures above the doors and fireplaces were painted by immigrant or visiting Dutch artists. The most distinguished was Willem van de Velde the Younger (1633–1707), who painted the four sea-pieces, dated 1673, in the Duchess's Bedchamber. He and his father had but

---

[1]The modern word *sash* (as applied to window-frames) is a corruption of *chassis* (or *chassee*, as the Duke spells it). It could be used to denote any kind of wooden window-frame, including the sliding frame, which at this time was gradually supplanting the casement. The fact that brass pulleys were fitted implies that the sashes were of the type that slide up and down.

recently come to England and were employed by Charles II, the father 'for taking and making draughts of sea-fights', the son 'to paint his father's drawings in colours'.

The majority of the other inset paintings are the work of two minor Dutch artists. The 1683 inventory reveals that no fewer than nineteen were painted by Dirck van den Bergen (1640–95), doubtless in the course of a visit he made to London in about 1674. He was a pupil of Adriaen van de Velde, whose style he somewhat slavishly imitated. His pastoral scenes with figures of peasants and cattle, coarsely painted, but suffused with a pleasant golden glow, are easily recognized in several of the first-floor rooms.

Fourteen other inset paintings are by Abraham Begeyn, also called Bega, (1637–97), another Dutchman who is known to have visited London in the early seventies. He painted pastoral landscapes, harbours and mountains, and also studies of plants and small animals.

Two minor immigrant Dutchmen who did work for Ham were Thomas Wyck (1616–77) and his son Jan (1640–1702). According to Walpole, Thomas's 'best pieces were representations of chymists and their laboratories which . . . were in compliment to the fashion at court, Charles II and Prince Rupert having each their laboratory.' Two of his 'chymists' surrounded with retorts, alligator skins and such

customary paraphernalia are in the Duke's Closet. But Wyck had also a contemporary vogue as a painter of 'views' and landscapes. When in England he particularly favoured the scenery of Thames-side, but at Ham he is represented by views of foreign seaports, fancifully rendered and garish in tone. The younger Wyck, on the other hand, specialized in horses and battles; and Sir Godfrey Kneller was not above employing him to paint them when required in the background of his own portraits. One of his battlepieces is in the Duke's Dressing Room.

The two inset paintings in the Duchess's Private Closet are assigned in the 1683 inventory to William Gowe Ferguson (1632/3-after 1695). A Scot by birth, he worked a long time in Holland and is usually counted among the artists of the Dutch school, whose manner of painting flowers and still life he adopted. According to Walpole, he also went to Italy 'where he composed two pictures . . . representing bas reliefs, antique stones, etc., on which the light was thrown in a surprising manner.' The examples of his work at Ham accord well with this description. Ferguson won little recognition and Walpole remarked that 'he worked very cheap.' His pictures are scarce in England, but there is one of similar character to those at Ham in the National Gallery of Scotland, and he is represented in several North European collections.

Apart from the Van de Veldes, none of these inset pictures is of much consequence; but together they form an interesting small repository of minor Dutch paintings of the period.

Among portrait painters Sir Peter Lely (1618–80), the most fashionable artist of Charles II's reign, is, as one would expect, strongly represented. His early portrait of the Duchess as a young woman is among his most attractive works. At least 8 of the 22 portraits in the Long Gallery are by him, while several others were painted under his immediate influence. Apart from Lely the most interesting 17th century portrait painters are Cornelius Johnson (1593–1664?) and John Michael Wright (1617–?1700); while Edmund Ashfield's portrait of the Duke (in the Duchess's Bedchamber) is among the few examples extant of this pastellist's work. There are also a few fine early miniatures, notably a 'Queen Elizabeth I' by Hilliard and the emblematic picture of an unknown young man against a background of flames by Oliver. The collection includes a number of 17th century copies after famous paintings and these seem to have been highly prized. For instance, the inset chosen to go over the chimneypiece in the Queen's Bedchamber—the most important room in the house—was not an original but a copy after Andrea del Sarto.

The early 18th century is represented by Sir Godfrey Kneller and by John Vanderbank. The most characteristic of the 'Knellers' is the portrait of Henrietta Cavendish in riding costume with her horse and groom in the background (Great Hall). There is a similar portrait of Henrietta, Countess of Oxford, at Welbeck Abbey. Vanderbank was another immigrant, who in the thirties, according to Vertue, 'had a great run of business, painting persons of quality.'

Ham is not rich in works of the golden age of English portraiture, though Reynolds's full-length portrait of Charlotte Walpole (pl. 33) and the interesting copies by Constable after Reynolds and Hoppner deserve mention. A rather fuller account of the pictures in each room will be found in the Tour of the House (p. 10). Certain paintings by unidentified artists, however, are passed over, as of minor interest.

LATER HISTORY OF THE HOUSE

After her husband's death in 1682, the Duchess continued to reside at Ham, but, as she suffered from gout, she was often away taking the waters at Tunbridge Wells and Bath. She was absent on one of these excursions in 1688 when William III landed in England. Before James fled the country, William sent him a letter (still among the muniments in the House of Lords), recommending him 'for the greater quiet of the City and for the greater safety of his person that he doe remove to Ham, where he shall be attended by the Guards who will be ready to preserve him from any Disturbance'; but James rejected the proposal on the pretext that 'Ham was a very ill winter house, and now unfurnished.'

At the Duchess's death in 1698, Ham became the property of Lionel Tollemache, 3rd Earl of Dysart, her son by her first marriage (she had no children by the Duke). As his mother's extravagances had left the estate encumbered, there was need of careful management; but the economies practised by the new Earl were drastic in the extreme, and were continued long after they had ceased to be necessary. In the words of Humphrey Prideaux,[1] the orientalist, who praised Lord Dysart's sense and prudence, 'that frugal and sparing way of living which his circumstances at first made necessary hath habituated him to that which, now he is out of those circumstances, is downright stinginess.' All accounts agree that the son was as miserly as the mother had been prodigal.

[1] H. Prideaux, *Letters to John Ellis*, 20 July 1696.

In addition to the large estates inherited from his parents, he had possessed himself of a great fortune by marrying an heiress, Grace Wilbraham; yet under this parsimonious rule Ham House deteriorated sadly from its former splendour.

Mackey, the author of *A journey through England*, 1724, reported that 'the gardens are still well kept, but the House more neglected than one could expect from so great an Estate.' Mrs Manley, whose *Secret memoirs and manners of several persons of quality*, 1709, is full of thinly disguised portraits of her contemporaries, draws a scathing likeness of Lord Dysart. She introduces him to the reader early in the morning in the garden at Ham. 'There's an early Lord!' she exclaims, 'He comes out betimes to save any Body's Breakfasting with him at home . . . what think you are his contemplations? Not the study of Letters or Humanity . . ., but how to weigh out his Provision to his Family, to seal up his Oven, that the hungry Domesticks may not pinch wherewith to appease the Cravings of Nature, from his numbered Loaves . . . This sordid Count has besides a prodigious Bank of ready Money, near Fifty Thousand Crowns of annual Rent; yet is there neither Plenty at his Board, Fire in his Kitchin, not Provisions in the Larder: His Wardrobe has nothing to boast of but Antiquity.'

An inventory of the house made in 1727 corroborates this account; the luxurious appointments with which the house had been equipped under the Duchess were stored away and the rooms left almost bare; there is no mention of silver chimney-furniture or silver-mounted cabinets; iron implements and old cane chairs were now the order of the day. In the Great Hall, for example, the only contents were: '*A Press bed Bolster; 4 Blankets and a Rugg all old; 14 old Cane Chairs; 2 Cedar Forms; 1 Branch for 12 Candles; an Iron Grate Back and Tongs, a Picture over ye Chimney and Two Statues.*'

It was said that Lord Dysart treated his children with similar meanness. 'He suffered his daughters, like Roses, to fade ungathered because he can't find in his Heart, while he lives, to give them a Fortune worthy of their Birth.'[1] His son, who died before him, was kept in such ignorance and so short of money that he only consorted with 'rascally Footmen and Domesticks, lolling whole days out of an upper Window with one of the Former for his Companion, playing Tricks and laughing for their Diversion at those who passed along.'[1]

Lord Dysart died in 1727 at the age of seventy-nine and was succeeded by his grandson Lionel, the 4th Earl. Three years later the 4th Earl called in the architect, John James, to survey the building, which was apparently in an extremely bad state of repair. The bay windows on the North Front were reported to be 'entirely ruinous, and incapable of Repair—otherwise than by Rebuilding them' and the 'Rooms that are Set upon the Arcades' were said to be in a dangerous state 'on Acct. of the Sleaziness of the Peers intended for their Support'. Damp was seriously affecting the basement and roof and James recommended replacing the tiles with 'Cornish blew slate'. The sash windows installed by the Lauderdales were now said to be 'all unfit to stand' and many of the casements needed repairs. The frontispiece above the front door was said to be 'drawn off from the Wall, from the Bottom to the Top' and had 'gone so far as to endanger even pulling the Roof after it'. Presumably these and other necessary repairs listed by John James were put in hand shortly afterwards but only one relevant account is known to survive. This is a bill from James Morehouse, dated July 1755 to September 1756, for miscellaneous repairs to stonework on the North Front and in the Forecourt and for relaying the marble paving in the Chapel. The 4th Earl must have had the South Front bay windows rebuilt at about the same time. He was also responsible for ordering some sumptuous new furniture, which included the gilded x-frame chairs and sofas, various gilded pier-glasses and tables, the red and green velvet suite and the hall chairs and tables; a number of paintings, the Bradshaw tapestries and various other furnishings date from his time too. Much of

[1] Mrs Manley, *op. cit.*

33. *Charlotte Walpole, Countess of Dysart* by Sir Joshua Reynolds

the new furniture was probably supplied by George Nix of Covent Garden, whose bills for furniture and repairs at Ham between 1729 and 1734 total £430 13s 6d. However, if Horace Walpole is to be believed, the 4th Earl was hardly more amiable or more generous than his grandfather. 'There is in this world', wrote Walpole, 'particularly in my world, for he lives directly over against me across the water, a strange brute called Earl of Dysart'. So close-fisted was he that, when his son, who wished to marry, asked for help, 'all the answer he could ever get was that the Earl could not afford, as he has five younger children, to make any settlement, and he offered, as a proof of his inability and kindness, to lend his son a large sum of money at low interest. This indigent usurer has thirteen thousand pounds a-year and sixty thousand pounds in the Funds.'

Notwithstanding his father's denial, the young man made a proposal of marriage to Walpole's niece, Charlotte (pl. 33), the illegitimate daughter of Sir Edward Walpole. 'Vidit, Venit, Vicit', wrote Walpole, 'the young Lord has liked her some time; on Saturday se'nnight he came to my brother and made his demand. The Princess did not know him by sight, but did not dislike him when she did; she consented, and they were to be married this morning.' According to Walpole, she unburdened herself to her sister thus: 'If I was but nineteen I would refuse point blank. I do not like to be married in a week to a man I never saw. But I am two-and twenty. Some people say I am handsome, some say I am not. I believe the truth is that I am likely to be large and go off soon. It is dangerous to refuse so great a match.'

As to her beauty, the visitor will be able to decide for himself from Reynolds's portrait in the Great Hall. Walpole was devoted to his niece, 'a more faultless being exists not within my knowledge.'

Her husband had succeeded to the title in 1770 as the 5th Earl. He was of a retiring disposition and could not endure visitors. It is related that when George III, curious to see the celebrated house, invited himself over from Windsor, his messenger returned with the reply that 'Whenever my house becomes a public spectacle, His Majesty shall certainly have the first view.' Horace Walpole also testified to the difficulty of gaining access to the grounds; the description of his first visit to Ham after his niece's installation deserves to be quoted, since it shows how little the atmosphere of the house has changed since 1770; already at that date it was redolent of past times.

'I went yesterday to see my niece in her new principality of Ham. It delighted me and made me peevish. Close to the Thames, in the centre of all rich and verdant beauty, it is so blocked up and barricaded with walls, vast trees, and gates, that you think yourself an hundred miles off and an hundred years back. The old furniture is so magnificently ancient, dreary and decayed, that at every step one's spirits sink, and all my passion for antiquity could not keep them up. Every minute I expected to see ghosts sweeping by; ghosts I would not give sixpence to see, Lauderdales, Talmachs, and Maitlands. There is an old brown gallery full of Vandycks and Lelys, charming miniatures, delightful Wouvermans, and Polenburghs, china, japan, bronzes, ivory cabinets, and silver dogs, pokers, bellows, etc., without end. One pair of bellows is of filigree. In this state of pomp and tatters my nephew intends it shall remain, and is so religious an observer of the venerable rites of his house, that because the gates never were opened by his father but once for the late Lord Granville, you are locked out and locked in, and after journeying all round the house as you do round an old French fortified town, you are at last admitted through the stableyard to creep along a dark passage by the housekeepers' room, and so by a back-door into the great hall.'

Although twice married, the 5th Earl died childless (in 1799) and was succeeded by his brother Wilbraham. When he in turn died without issue (in 1821), the Tollemache family became extinct in the male line, and the title devolved upon his only surviving sister Louisa, who became Countess of Dysart in her own right. She was succeeded in 1840 by her grandson, the 8th Earl; the 9th Earl, who died

34. Mid-19th century view of the North Front

in 1935, was his grandson. On Lord Dysart's death, Ham House became the property of his kinsmen Sir Lyonel Tollemache, Bt, and Mr Cecil Tollemache, who generously presented it to the National Trust.

BIBLIOGRAPHY

BRAY, W., see under MANNING, O.

BRAYLEY, E., *A topographical history of Surrey*, London, 1841.

BURNET, G., Bishop of Salisbury, *History of his own time*, 1723–24.

CRIPPS, D., *Elizabeth of the Sealed Knot*, Roundwood Press, Kineton, 1975.

DUNBAR, J. 'The building activities of the Duke and Duchess of Lauderdale, 1670–82', *Archaeological Journal*, vol. 132, for 1975.

EDWARDS, R., and RAMSEY, L. G. G., *The Stuart Period, 1603–1714*, The Connoisseur Period Guides, London, 1957.

HILL, O., and CORNFORTH, J., *English Country Houses, Caroline, 1625–1685*, London, 1966.

JOURDAIN, M., 'Dutch Influence on English Post-Restoration Furniture' in *Country Life*, vol. lix, 1926, p. 474.

LYSONS, D., *The environs of London*, London, 1792.

MACKENZIE, W. C., *The life and times of John Maitland, Duke of Lauderdale*, London, 1923.

MANNING, O., and BRAY, W., *The history and antiquities of the County of Surrey*, London, 1804.

MARILLIER, H. C., *English tapestry in the 18th century*, London, 1930.

ROUNDELL, Mrs C., *Ham House, its history and art treasures*, London, 1904.

TIPPING, H. A., *English homes*, period iv., vol. 1, London, 1920.

TIPPING, H. A., Articles on Ham House in *Country Life*, vol. xlvii, 1920, pp. 372, 404, 410, 440.

TIPPING, H. A., 'Chimney furniture at Ham House' in *Country Life*, vol. xlvii, 1920, p. 448.

TOLLEMACHE, Maj-Gen. E., *The Tollemaches of Helmingham and Ham*, 1949.

Guided tours of the house can be arranged. To avoid congestion parties have to be limited to a maximum of 30 people but more than one group can be taken round at the same time if necessary. A charge of £2 is made for the services of each guide-escort, payable on arrival. (School parties pay no charge). Application should be made to the Department of Furniture and Woodwork, Victoria and Albert Museum, London SW7 2RL.

As an experiment and as part of our endeavour to make the workings of this historic house more understandable certain rooms that are largely unfurnished and are not part of the normal tour of the house are to be made available for viewing by prior appointment only. These rooms include the Bathroom, Kitchen and Dairy, as well as the Ice-House. A maximum of 8 persons will be allowed at any one time in these special areas. Application should be made to the Resident Officer, Ham House, Richmond, Surrey TW10 7RS. (tel. 01-940 1950).

HOURS OF OPENING

Summer

(April to September): Sundays, Tuesdays, Wednesdays and Bank Holidays 14.00 to 18.00.

Winter

(October to March): Sundays, Tuesdays, Wednesdays and Bank Holidays 12.00 to 16.00.
Closed Good Friday, 24, 25, 26 December and 1 January.

Children under 12 must be accompanied by an adult. Members of the National Trust are admitted free on production of current membership cards.

TRANSPORT

Underground (District Line) or British Railways (from Waterloo or Broad Street Station) to Richmond Station; Buses nos. 65 and 71 Richmond Station–Kingston. Alight at Fox and Duck Inn, Petersham.
Green Line Routes. (Alight at Dysart Arms, Petersham).

714 via Baker Street, Hyde Park Corner, Richmond–Kingston.
716 via North Finchley, Hyde Park Corner, Richmond–Kingston.
716A via North Finchley, Hyde Park Corner, Richmond–Kingston.

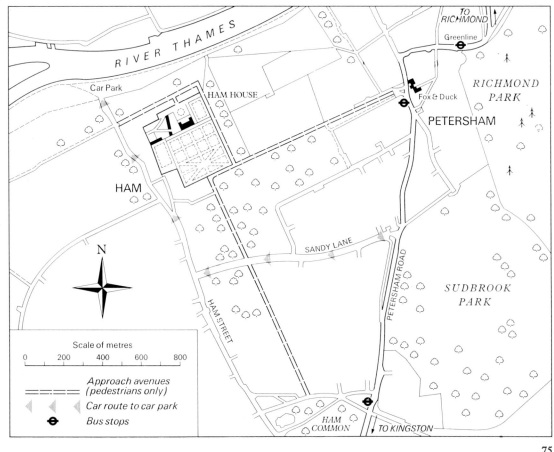

RIVER THAMES

Car Park

HAM HOUSE

HAM

TO RICHMOND

Greenline

RICHMOND PARK

Fox & Duck

PETERSHAM

N

SANDY LANE

PETERSHAM ROAD

SUDBROOK PARK

HAM STREET

Scale of metres

| 0 | 200 | 400 | 600 | 800 |

——— Approach avenues (pedestrians only)

◄ ◄ Car route to car park

⬤ Bus stops

HAM COMMON

TO KINGSTON